The Best Fries Cookbook

40 Recipes to Celebrate the World's Favorite Food!

By

Martha Stone

License Notes

No part of this Book can be reproduced in any form or by any means including print, electronic, scanning or photocopying unless prior permission is granted by the author.

All ideas, suggestions and guidelines mentioned here are written for informative purposes. While the author has taken every possible step to ensure accuracy, all readers are advised to follow information at their own risk. The author cannot be held responsible for personal and/or commercial damages in case of misinterpreting and misunderstanding any part of this Book.

Table of Contents

Introduction

French fries may very well be America's favorite food but did you know that they originate from Belgium?

Historians reveal that the first potato strips hit the oil in the 17th century in Belgium's Meuse Valley. Apparently, when the river froze over locals, instead of frying fish, would use the humble potato as a substitute.

In fact, it wasn't' until 1801 that French fries arrived in the USA.

Today, the average American eats nearly 30 pounds of fries, every year.

The Brits sprinkle their chips with salt and vinegar, the Belgians dip their French fries in mayonnaise, and the Dutch eat their frites with peanut butter.

But however you serve them or whatever you call them; chips, fries, French fries or frites; they are one of the most beloved foods on the planet!

The Best French Fries Cookbook gives you 40 simple but unique and creative recipes for French Fries for you to prepare at home.

Asian Fries

East meets West as Thai flavorings add zest, spice, and flavor to these crispy French fries.

Servings: 3-4

Total Time: 1hour 45mins

Ingredients:

- 1 tbsp peanut oil
- 1 tbsp freshly squeezed lime juice
- 1 tbsp fish sauce
- 1 tbsp smooth peanut butter
- ¼ tsp salt
- ¼ tsp pepper
- 1½ tsp garlic (peeled, minced)
- ½ tsp coriander powder
- ½ tsp cayenne pepper
- ½ tsp onion powder
- ½ tsp ground cumin
- 3 medium potatoes (washed, skin-on, cut into ¼ "fries)
- Vegetable oil

Directions:

1. In a ziplock bag, combine the peanut oil with the freshly squeezed lime juice, fish sauce, peanut butter, salt, pepper, garlic, coriander, cayenne, onion powder, and cumin.

2. Add the fries to the bag and gently shake to combine, making sure the fries are all coated. Set the bag to one side to marinate for 60 minutes.

3. Preheat the main oven to 400 degrees F.

4. Pour a drop of vegetable oil onto an aluminum lined baking sheet and using kitchen paper wipe to cover the whole sheet.

5. Arrange the fries, in a single layer on the sheet, making sure they don't touch one another and bake in the oven for between 40-45 minutes, flipping over a couple of times during the cooking process.

Avocado Ranch Fries

Soft, and creamy avocado fries with a crispy panko coating, melt in the mouth. Serve with spicy ranch dip for a flavor sensation.

Servings: 4

Total Time: 30mins

Ingredients:

- ½ medium lime (juiced)
- ½ cup ranch dressing
- ½ cup panko breadcrumbs

- 3 ripe avocados (peeled, pitted, sliced into 'fries')
- Sea salt
- Black pepper
- Olive oil
- Hot sauce

Directions:

1. Preheat the main oven to 400 degrees F. Cover a cookie sheet with parchment.

2. Add the lime juice and half of the ranch dressing to a small bowl. Stir to combine.

3. Add the breadcrumbs to a separate bowl.

4. Dip each avocado 'fry' in the lime/ranch mixture and then dip in breadcrumbs to coat. Arrange on the cookie sheet.

5. Season well with sea salt and black pepper, drizzle with a little olive oil.

6. Place in the oven and bake for 20 minutes.

7. Add the remaining ranch to a bowl and add a few shakes of hot sauce. Stir well. Serve the avocado fries with the spicy ranch.

Banh Mi French Fries

This dish is tasty and satisfying enough to serve as a main meal. Bursting with flavor and texture it's sure to become a new favorite.

Servings: 2

Total Time: 1hour 15mins

Ingredients:

Pickled Carrots and Daikon:

- 1 large carrot (julienned)
- 2" piece of daikon (julienned)
- ½ tsp salt
- 2 tsp sugar

Fries:

- 1 large russet potato (peeled, cut into ⅛" fries)
- Grapeseed oil (to fry)
- Salt and black pepper
- ½ cup ready-made Chinese BBQ pork (coarsely chopped)
- ½ cup pickled daikons and carrots
- 1 jalapeno (sliced)
- ½ cup cilantro (roughly chopped)
- Mayo and sriracha (to serve)

Directions:

1. Prepare the pickles; add the carrots and pickled daikons to a mixing bowl, sprinkle with salt and sugar and set to one side to rest for 15 minutes. Rinse the pickled veggies, drain thoroughly and transfer to the fridge until needed.

2. Now prepare the fries. Soak the fries for 20 minutes, in a bowl of iced water, remembering to swirl around every few minutes. Rinse under cold running tap water, and using kitchen paper, pat dry before frying.

3. Over a moderately high heat, heat 1" of oil in a deep sided pot or pan until it registers 350 degrees F on a thermometer.

4. Arrange a wire rack inside a rimmed baking sheet.

5. Working in small batches, carefully drop the fries into the deep pan.

6. Using a slotted utensil, stir every few seconds to ensure they evenly brown.

7. As soon as the fries are golden, after around 4 minutes, remove from the hot oil and carefully drain on the rack. Continue with the cooking process until all of the potatoes are used.

8. Increase the temperature of the oil to 375 degrees F and carefully, taking care not to splash yourself, add the cooked fries to the pan, to make them crunchy and brown, 1-2 minutes.

9. Drain the fries and season to taste.

10. Top with the Chinese BBQ pork, pickled carrot and daikon, sliced jalapeno, cilantro, mayo and sriracha.

11. Enjoy.

BBQ Pulled Pork Fries

Shoestring fries are topped with tender pulled pork, melting cheese, and tangy BBQ sauce. The ultimate side dish for any cookout!

Servings: 8-10

Total Time: 1hour

Ingredients:

- 1 (32 ounce) bag frozen shoestring fries
- 1 (8 ounce) container pulled pork
- 1 cup Colby Jack cheese (shredded)

- ½ onion (peeled, finely chopped)
- 1 large plum tomato (finely chopped)
- 1 bunch scallions (thinly sliced)
- 1 (18 ounce) jar BBQ sauce

Directions:

1. Cook the fries on a baking sheet according to bag directions.

2. Use a large spatula to flip the fries so that the crisp side faces are facing down.

3. Top with the pulled pork.

4. Sprinkle with the shredded cheese, followed by the onion, tomato, and scallions. Place back in the hot oven and cook for several minutes, until the pork is heated through and the cheese is melting.

5. Drizzle with a generous amount of BBQ sauce before serving.

Belgian Fries with Creamy Sauce Andalouse

Belgian fries are typically served with a mayonnaise-based sauce.

Servings: 4-6

Total Time: 1hour 30mins

Ingredients:

Sauce:

- 1 cup full-fat mayonnaise
- 2 tbsp tomato paste
- 2 tbsp onion (peeled, finely chopped)
- 1 tbsp each of red and green bell pepper (finely chopped)
- 1 tbsp freshly squeezed lemon juice
- ¼ tsp salt

Fries:

- 5-6 cups vegetable or canola oil (to fry)
- 3 pounds russet baking potatoes (peeled, cut into ⅓" fries)
- Salt and black pepper

Directions:

1. To make the sauce combine the mayonnaise, with the tomato paste, onion, bell peppers, lemon juice and salt. Stir to combine, cover and transfer to the fridge to chill for a minimum of 60 minutes. Remove from fridge and bring to room temperature before serving.

2. In a heavy pan, heat 2" of oil, over a moderately low heat until the thermometer reads 300 degrees F.

3. Make the fries: Heat 2" of oil slowly in a 5-6 quart heavy pot over moderately low heat until a thermometer registers 300 degrees F.

4. While the oil is heating submerge the fries in a large bowl of iced water.

5. In a bowl, rinse the potatoes, changing the water several times until the water is totally clear.

6. Drain the potatoes, using a colander and arrange in a single layer on numerous layers of kitchen paper, pat dry.

7. When the oil reaches 300 degrees F increase heat to medium high and in batches of four, fry the potatoes, flipping until cooked through, this will take a few minutes.

8. In between batches return the oil to a heat of 300 degrees F.

9. Using a slotted utensil, remove the fries and place on kitchen paper to cool for half an hour.

10. Reheat the oil over medium high heat until the temperature reads 375 degrees F.

11. In batches of four, flipping, fry the cooked potatoes for 3-4 minutes, until golden while returning the oil to 375 degrees in between batches.

12. Transfer to kitchen paper to drain, then season.

13. Serve with the dipping sauce.

Breakfast French Fries with Sausage Gravy

This breakfast or brunch of champions is sure to set you up for the whole day.

Servings: 4

Total Time: 35mins

Ingredients:

- 1 (32 ounce) bag frozen fries
- 1½ cups Cheddar cheese (shredded, divided)
- ⅓ pound breakfast sausage (casings removed)
- 2 tbsp all-purpose flour
- 1 cup whole milk
- Kosher salt
- Freshly ground black pepper
- Pinch of cayenne pepper
- 1 tbsp virgin olive oil
- 4 large, organic eggs
- Chives (to garnish)

Directions:

1. Bake the frozen fries according to the package directions.

2. Preheat the main oven to 350 degrees F.

3. In an ovenproof pan or skillet, add in a single layer, around ⅓ of the cooked fries.

4. Top with ⅓ of the cheese. Repeat the process another two times with the remaining fries and cheese. Cook in the preheated oven until the fries are super crispy and the cheese melts, this will take between 12-15 minutes.

5. Now make the gravy. In a medium-sized pan over moderate heat, cook the sausage until browned on all sides.

6. Sprinkle the flour over the sausage and cook for 60 seconds.

7. Pour the milk on the sausage and bring to a boil. Reduce the heat and simmer for 4-6 minutes, until the mixture thickens.

8. Season with cayenne, salt, and pepper and remove the pan from the heat.

9. In a large pan or skillet over moderate heat, heat the olive oil.

10. Break the eggs into the pan, and pour in approximately 2 tsp of water.

11. Cover the pan with a lid and cook until the whites are totally set, this will take around 3-4 minutes.

12. Place the eggs on top of the fries, along with the sausage gravy and garnish with chives.

Canadian Fries with Gravy and Cheddar Curds (Poutine)

When you have the munchies, nothing fits the bill better than Poutine. This Canadian dish of French fries, gravy and cheese curds has to be the best comfort food ever.

Servings: 4-6

Total Time: 3hours

Ingredients:

- 4 pounds russet potatoes (rinsed, skin on, patted dry, cut into ¼"fries)
- 4 tbsp unsalted butter
- ¼ cup flour
- 1 shallot (minced)
- 1 garlic clove (peeled, minced)
- 4 cups beef stock
- 1 tbsp cider vinegar
- 2 tbsp tomato ketchup
- 1 tbsp whole green peppercorns
- ½ tsp Worcestershire sauce
- Sea salt
- Black pepper
- Vegetable oil (to fry)
- 2 cups cheddar cheese curds

Directions:

1. Place the fries in a mixing bowl and add sufficient cold water to totally cover. Transfer to the fridge for approximately 2-3 hours.

2. In the meantime, over moderately high heat, in a saucepan, melt the butter.

3. Add the flour and while stirring, cook for a couple of minutes, until smooth.

4. Next, add the shallot followed by the garlic and continue cooking until softened, this will only take 2-3 minutes.

5. Add the stock, cider vinegar, ketchup, green peppercorns, Worcestershire sauce, a pinch of salt and a dash of pepper, and bring to the boil. Continue cooking for 6-8 minutes until thickened. Take the pan off the heat and keep the gravy warm.

6. Add the oil to a large Dutch oven of no less than 6 quarts. The oil needs to be approximately 3" deep. Over a moderate heat, heat until a frying thermometer registers 325 degrees F.

7. Drain the fries, and using kitchen paper, thoroughly dry.

8. Working in relatively small batches, add the fries and fry, while occasionally tossing until fork tender but crisp, this will take around 5 minutes.

9. Drain the fries on kitchen paper and set aside to cool for half an hour.

10. Increase, the temperature to moderately high and heat the oil until it registers 375 degrees F.

11. Working in relatively small batches, place the fries back in the oil and fry, occasionally tossing, until golden and crisp, about 3 minutes.

12. Transfer the French fries to kitchen paper to briefly drain, and divide between individual bowls.

13. Pour the gravy over the French fries, and add the cheddar curds.

14. Serve and enjoy.

Cajun French Fries

You don't have to travel to the Deep South to enjoy these seasoned fries.

Servings: 4

Total Time: 1hour

Ingredients:

- 4 large baking potatoes (scrubbed, cut into fries)
- 2-4 tsp Cajun seasoning (to taste)
- 1 tbsp olive oil
- Sea salt
- Black pepper

Directions:

1. Transfer the fries to a bowl of ice water.

2. Preheat the main oven to 425 degrees F.

3. As soon as the oven reaches temperature, drain the water from the fries, and using kitchen paper towel, pat dry.

4. Place the fries in a bowl, scatter with Cajun seasoning (the amount is dependent on your taste) and drizzle with olive oil. Using clean fingers evenly combine the oil with the fries.

5. Place the fries on a lightly greased baking sheet and bake in the oven for half an hour, until golden and fork-tender, remember to frequently turn to ensure an even bake.

6. Season with sea salt and black pepper.

Cheesy Garlic Fries with Spring Onions

Melted cheese on crispy fries sprinkled with spring onions in just half an hour.

Servings: 4

Total Time: 30mins

Ingredients:

- 1 (16 ounce) bag frozen French fries
- Virgin olive oil
- Kosher salt
- Black pepper
- 3 garlic cloves (peeled, minced)
- 1 cup Monterey Jack cheese (shredded)
- 2 green onions (sliced)

Directions:

1. Preheat your grill to moderately high heat.

2. Using aluminum foil, make four large rectangles. Divide the fries into four, and spread each portion of fries out, onto each of the four sheets.

3. Drizzle with oil and toss with kosher salt and black pepper.

4. Fold each rectangle crosswise in half and seal to make parcels.

5. When the grill is sufficiently hot, cook the aluminum foil parcels, occasionally tossing and turning, for approximately 15-20 minutes, or until golden and heated through.

6. Open each of the parcels and sprinkle with minced garlic. Toss to coat, and with the foil open, allow to grill for a further 60 seconds; this will help the fries to crisp.

7. Scatter with shredded cheese and continue grilling until the cheese melts.

8. Remove and sprinkle with green onions.

Cheesy Bacon Fries

Sometimes you just can't beat the winning combination of cheese and bacon, especially when served with fresh scallions and ranch dip.

Servings: 8

Total Time: 50mins

Ingredients:

- 1 (32 ounce) bag frozen French fries
- 2 cups Cheddar cheese (grated)
- ½ cup scallions (thinly sliced)
- ¼ cup cooked bacon bits
- Ranch dressing (to serve)

Directions:

1. Prepare the French fries according to the directions on the bag.

2. Preheat your oven's broiler.

3. Transfer the cooked fries to a baking sheet.

4. Scatter the grated cheese, scallions, and bacon bits over the fries.

5. Pop under the broiler for 2-3 minutes, until the cheese melts.

6. Serve straight away with ranch dressing for dipping.

Cheesy Fries with Caramelized Onions and Thousand Island Dressing

Lots of flavor in this easy to prepare dish thanks to the tangy Thousand Island dressing, sweet caramelized onions, and creamy cheese sauce.

Servings: 4

Total Time: 45mins

Ingredients:

Caramelized Onions:

- 3 cup onions (peeled, sliced)
- 2 tbsp butter

Fries:

- 1 (20 ounce) bag frozen French fries
- 1 cup store-bought cheese sauce (any brand)
- 1 cup Thousand Island dressing (any brand)
- 1 cup caramelized onions (finely diced)
- Parsley (chopped, to garnish)

Directions:

1. To caramelize the onions; in a pan over moderate heat, cook the onions, while frequently stirring in the butter until dark brown, this will take around 25-30 minutes. Set to one side until you are ready to use.

2. Preheat the main oven to 400 degrees F. Using parchment paper line a cookie sheet.

3. Arrange the fries on the sheet in an even, single layer and cook according to the package directions.

4. In the meantime, and while the fries cook, warm the cheese sauce in a pan over moderate heat.

5. As soon as the fries are sufficiently cooked, pour the warmed sauce over the top of the French fries.

6. Spoon the dressing and caramelized onions over the top of the cheese sauce and garnish with parsley.

Chili Lime Fries

Bursting with zesty, spicy flavor, these zingy fries are the ultimate game-day snack.

Servings: 4

Total Time: 50mins

Ingredients:

- 2 russet potatoes (peeled, cut into fries)
- 2 tbsp olive oil
- Juice of 2 medium limes
- 1½ tsp hot chili powder
- 1 tsp sea salt
- ¼ tsp cayenne pepper

Directions:

1. Preheat your oven to 450 degrees F. Cover a baking sheet with a parchment paper.

2. Place the potatoes onto the baking sheet. Then drizzle over the oil and lime juice.

3. Sprinkle with the chili, sea salt, and cayenne.

4. Place in the oven and bake for 45 minutes.

5. Enjoy!

Cinnamon Sweet Potato French Fries

Cinnamon and sweet potatoes are a winning combination.

Servings: 4-6

Total Time: 1hour 5mins

Ingredients:

- ⅓ cup extra virgin olive oil
- 2 large sweet potatoes (peeled, cut into ¼" fries)
- Salt
- 3 tsp ground cinnamon

Directions:

1. Preheat the main oven to 350 degrees F.

2. Using parchment paper, line a jelly roll pan.

3. In a bowl, combine the olive oil with the fries, and toss to combine.

4. Arrange the fries on the parchment paper and season with salt.

5. Sprinkle 1½ tsp of cinnamon over the fries and bake in the oven for 20 minutes before turning over and sprinkling with more salt and cinnamon.

6. Bake in the oven for another half an hour.

7. Serve.

Clam Chowder Crinkle Fries

Crinkle- cut fries topped with creamy, thick clam chowder, Cheddar cheese, and fresh herbs are a comforting weekend treat, guaranteed to lift your spirits.

Servings: 6-8

Total Time: 1hour 10mins

Ingredients:

- 1 (26 ounce) bag frozen crinkle-cut fries
- 8 ounces clam chowder soup
- Sea salt and black pepper
- ½ cup sharp Cheddar cheese (grated)
- 3 rashers bacon (cooked, crumbled)
- ¼ cup fresh chives (chopped)
- ¼ cup fresh parsley (chopped)

Directions:

1. Preheat the main oven to 350 degrees F.

2. Cook the crinkle fries according to bag directions. When the fries are nearly ready, heat the chowder in a saucepan.

3. Preheat the oven's broiler.

4. Transfer the cooked fries to a large baking dish, season with sea salt and black pepper. Pour the chowder over the fries and sprinkle with cheese.

5. Place under the broiler for 5-6 minutes until the cheese melts.

6. Scatter over the crumbled bacon, fresh chives, and parsley.

7. Serve!

Crispy Beet Fries

Sweet, crunchy beetroot fries are sprinkled with sea salt flakes for a yummy, lighter alternative to potato fries. A great afternoon snack!

Servings: 2

Total Time: 35mins

Ingredients:

- 2 large beetroots (peeled, chopped into medium-thick 'fries')
- 1 tbsp virgin coconut oil
- ½ tsp sea salt flakes
- Pinch chili flakes

Directions:

1. Preheat the main oven to 375 degrees F. Cover a baking sheet with parchment.

2. Add the beet fries to a large bowl, drizzle with coconut oil and sprinkle with sea salt flakes. Toss well to coat and transfer to a baking sheet.

3. Place in the oven and bake for just under half an hour. Rotate the sheet halfway through cooking.

4. Season with chili flakes and serve!

Dutch Frites with Peanut Sauce

No ketchup required. In Holland, the Dutch love their fries with creamy, rich mayonnaise and peanut sauce.

Servings: 4

Total Time: 30mins

Ingredients

Peanut Sauce:

- ½ cup crunchy peanut butter
- ¼ cup coconut milk
- 2 tbsp soy sauce
- 2 tbsp freshly squeezed lime juice
- 1 tbsp runny honey
- 1 tsp fresh ginger (peeled, minced)
- 1 tsp garlic (peeled, minced)
- 1 tsp fish sauce
- 1 tsp chili-garlic sauce

Dutch Frites:

- 1 bag (23 ounce) straight cut fries
- 2 tsp lime zest (finely grated)
- ¼ cup mayonnaise
- ¼ cup white onion (peeled, finely chopped)
- 2 tbsp roasted peanuts (roughly chopped)

Directions

1. First, make the peanut sauce. In a bowl, whisk together the peanut butter, coconut milk, soy sauce, freshly squeezed lime juice, honey, ginger, garlic, fish sauce and chili sauce. If you feel the sauce is a little thick, add 1 tablespoon of water, until you achieve your preferred consistency.

2. Prepare the pack of fries according to the package instructions. When cooked, transfer to a bowl and sprinkle with the lime zest, tossing to combine.

3. Transfer to a serving platter, drizzle with mayo and top with peanut sauce.

4. Garnish with chopped onion and roasted peanuts.

Eggs Benedict Fries

This brunchtime, instead of boring bread why not enjoy creamy hollandaise sauce and a delicately poached egg on top of golden fries?

Servings: 3-4

Total Time: 45mins

Ingredients:

- 1 (12 ounce) bag frozen French fries
- 1 cup hollandaise sauce
- 2 poached eggs
- Fresh chives (finely chopped)
- Pinch smoked paprika

Directions:

1. Cook the fries according to bag directions.

2. When the fries are nearly cooked, gently heat the hollandaise sauce in a small saucepan.

3. Arrange the cooked fries in a pile on a serving plate. Pour over the hot hollandaise sauce and arrange the poached eggs on top.

4. Scatter over the chives and sprinkle with a little paprika.

5. Serve!

Feta Cheese Fries and Roasted Garlic Saffron Aioli

Homemade roasted garlic with fresh saffron aioli is as good as any restaurant appetizer.

Servings: 2-4

Total Time: 1hour 30mins

Ingredients:

Roasted Garlic:

- 6 cloves of garlic
- Olive oil
- Garlic Saffron Aioli:
- ½ cup mayonnaise
- 1 tbsp Dijon mustard
- Roasted garlic
- Generous pinch of saffron
- 1-2 tbsp freshly squeezed lemon juice
- Salt and pepper (to season)

Fries:

- 4 russet potatoes (cut into ¼ "fries)
- ¼ cup olive oil
- 1 tsp fresh oregano
- 1 tsp fresh basil
- Pinch cayenne pepper
- Salt and pepper (to season)
- Fresh parsley (to garnish)
- 6 ounces feta cheese (crumbled)

Directions:

1. Preheat the main oven to 400 degrees F.

2. Start by roasting the garlic. First cut the top part of the garlic off. Peel off any excess skin from the garlic bulb.

3. Arrange the garlic cloves on a sheet of aluminum foil and lightly drizzle with 1 tsp of the olive oil.

4. Cover with aluminum foil and bake in the oven, until soft and browned, this will take approximately 40 minutes.

5. Take the garlic out of the oven and set to one side to cool for 4-5 minutes.

6. Squeeze out the garlic into a small bowl, and using a fork, mash.

7. Reduce the temperature of the main oven to 425 degrees F.

8. Next, make the aioli. In a blender combine the mayonnaise with the mustard. Add the prepared roasted garlic, saffron, freshly squeezed lemon juice, a pinch of salt and a dash of pepper. Blend until combined and silky smooth.

9. Add the cut fries to a large mixing bowl and drizzle with olive oil.

10. Add the basil, oregano, cayenne, pepper and salt and gently toss to evenly coat.

11. Arrange the fries, in a single layer, on 2 baking sheets and bake in the oven for between 15-20 minutes. Reduce the heat to 400 degrees F, flip the fries over, and return to the oven for another 15-20 minutes, or until cooked through.

12. Take out of the oven and toss with fresh parsley and cheese.

13. Serve alongside the aioli.

Fries alla Carbonara

These French fries are delicious on their own or served with chicken; rich, creamy and very moreish.

Servings: 2

Total Time: 50mins

Ingredients:

- 1 pound potatoes (peeled, sliced)
- 3 ounces pancetta (diced)
- 2 tbsp olive oil
- Black pepper
- 3 tbsp pecorino cheese (grated)

Directions:

1. Preheat the main oven to 400 degrees F.

2. In a baking pan, combine the potatoes with the pancetta, oil and black pepper.

3. Arrange the pan on the middle oven rack and bake for between 30-40 minutes, or until the potatoes are cooked through and fork tender.

4. Remove from the oven and immediately scatter with grated cheese, and sprinkle with lots of black pepper.

5. Serve.

Garlic Crab French Fries with Aioli

A truly French way to jazz up frozen fries and a great appetizer or party food snack.

Servings: 2-4

Total Time: 45mins

Ingredients:

- 1 (32 ounces) bag frozen crinkle-cut fries
- ½ pound frozen crab

Butter:

- 2 tbsp virgin olive oil
- 2 tbsp butter
- 1 clove garlic (peeled, minced)

Aioli:

- 4 tbsp mayonnaise
- 4 tbsp sour cream
- 1 clove garlic (peeled, minced)
- Sea salt and black pepper

Directions:

1. First, cook the fries according to the manufacturer's instructions.

2. Cook the crab according to the package directions.

3. Crack the crab shells, and transfer the meat to a mixing bowl.

4. To prepare the garlic butter, add the oil, butter, and garlic to a microwave-safe bowl, and microwave for 25 seconds, until the butter melts. Set to one side while the fries are baking.

5. In a bowl, combine the mayonnaise with the sour cream, garlic, sea salt and black pepper and put the aioli to one side.

6. When the fries are baked, remove from the oven and place in a bowl.

7. Pour the garlic butter over the top of the fries and gently toss to combine.

8. Transfer to a serving platter. Season with sea salt.

9. Arrange the crab on top of the fries, drizzle with aioli and serve with the remaining aioli for dipping.

Green Bean Breaded Fries with Wasabi Dip

Veggies fries are a fun, new food-trend that we're totally into! Especially these crunchy, breaded green bean fries served with a spicy wasabi dip.

Servings: 4

Total Time: 40mins

Ingredients:

Fries:

- 2 tbsp olive oil
- 1½ cups breadcrumbs
- Sea salt and black pepper
- 2 tbsp whole milk
- 2 medium eggs
- ½ cup flour
- 1 pound fresh green beans (trimmed)

Dip:

- 1 cucumber (peeled, deseeded, diced)
- ½ cup ranch dressing
- 2 tsp powdered wasabi
- 1 tsp white vinegar

Directions:

1. Preheat the main oven to 425 degrees F. Cover a cookie sheet with parchment.

2. Combine the olive oil, breadcrumbs, sea salt, and black pepper in a shallow dish.

3. In a second shallow dish add the milk and eggs. Whisk to combine.

4. Finally, add the flour to a third bowl.

5. In batches, dunk the green beans in the flour, followed by the milk/egg, and finally the breadcrumbs. Arrange on the cookie sheet.

6. Place in the oven and bake for just over 20 minutes.

7. While the fries cook, prepare the dip.

8. Combine the cucumber, dressing, powdered wasabi, and vinegar in a small bowl.

9. Serve the cooked fries with the wasabi dip.

Italian Seasoned Chunky Fries

An Italian twist on these crispy homemade fries.

Servings: 4

Total Time: 45mins

Ingredients:

- Nonstick spray
- ¾ cup cornflake crumbs
- 6 tbsp Parmesan cheese (grated)
- 1½ tsp Italian herb seasoning
- 1⅓ pound potatoes (cut into ½" thick fries)
- 1 medium egg (lightly beaten)

Directions:

1. Preheat the main oven to 375 degrees F.

2. Lightly mist two baking trays with nonstick spray.

3. In a shallow mixing bowl, combine the crumbs with the grated cheese and herb seasoning. Set to one side.

4. Dip the fries into the lightly beaten egg, making sure you evenly coat with the cheese-herb crumb mixture, and in a single layer, arrange on the baking trays.

5. Bake in the preheated oven for 20 minutes, flip over and continue to cook for another 10-15 minutes, until the potatoes are crispy, browned and fork tender.

6. Serve.

Jicama French Fries

Jicamas, or Mexican potatoes as they are also called, are mild, crunchy and great to cook with.

Servings: 4

Total Time: 1hour

Ingredients:

- Sea salt
- 2 cups jicama (peeled, cut into fries)
- 2 tbsp avocado oil
- ¼ tsp garlic powder
- 1 tsp cumin
- 1 tsp smoked paprika

Directions:

1. Bring a lightly salted pan of water to boil.

2. Add the fries and boil for 10 minutes. Drain the fries using a colander and transfer to a mixing bowl.

3. Coat the fries with the oil, then season with ¼ tsp sea salt, garlic powder, cumin and paprika and blend in the spices.

4. Spread the fries evenly and in a single layer on an oiled baking pan and bake at 400 degrees F for half an hour, flip them over halfway through the cooking process. Cook until crisp.

Lemony Pepper Fries

So simple, yet so delicious. Fresh, zesty lemon and fiery black pepper fries are the perfect side order for so many different dishes.

Servings: 6

Total Time: 1 hour

Ingredients:

- 6 large potatoes (skin-on, cut into thin fries)
- ⅓ cup olive oil
- 1 tbsp sea salt
- 3 tbsp lemon pepper
- Zest of 3 medium lemons (finely grated)

Directions:

1. Preheat the main oven to 400 degrees F. Cover two cookie sheets with parchment.

2. Soak the potatoes in ice cold water for 20 minutes. Drain and pat dry.

3. Transfer the soaked fries to a large bowl and drizzle with oil. Sprinkle with salt and lemon pepper. Toss well to coat. Arrange on the baking sheets.

4. Place in the oven and bake for 35 minutes, rotating the baking sheets halfway through cooking.

5. Sprinkle with lemon zest, toss a final time and serve!

Loaded Cuban Fries

All the flavor of a loaded Cuban sandwich in a tasty plate of hot, cheesy fries. Yum!

Servings: 4

Total Time: 1 hour

Ingredients:

Fries:

- 1 (30 ounce) bag frozen French fries

Cheese Sauce:

- 3 tbsp salted butter
- 3 tbsp all-purpose flour
- 2 cups skim milk
- 8 ounces Swiss cheese (chopped)
- Salt and pepper

Toppings:

- ¼ cup dill pickles (diced)
- 1 cup ham (diced)
- ½ tbsp yellow mustard

Directions:

1. Cook the fries following the package directions.

2. When the fries are nearly cooked, begin preparing the sauce.

3. In a saucepan over moderate heat, melt the butter.

4. Whisk in the flour until lump-free followed by the milk.

5. Finally, add the Swiss cheese. Gently stir until the cheese has melted completely. Continue to cook until you have a thick sauce. Taste, and adjust the seasoning. Take off the heat.

6. Arrange the cooked fries on a serving plate, pour over the cheese sauce. Sprinkle with the pickles, ham, and a drizzle of mustard. Enjoy!

Low-Carb Carrot Fries with Chipotle Lime Mayo

Carrots are a low-carb alternative to potato making this a guilt-free way to help satisfy those French fry cravings.

Servings: 4

Total Time: 30mins

Ingredients:

Fries:

- 1 pound carrots (peeled, cut into fries)
- 2 tbsp olive oil
- ½ tsp ground cumin
- ½ tsp ground paprika
- Sea salt and black pepper

Chipotle Lime Mayo:

- 2 tsp jarred chopped chipotle pepper
- ⅓ cup low-fat mayo
- Juice of ½ a medium lime

Directions:

1. Preheat the main oven to 425 degrees F. Cover a baking sheet with parchment.

2. Add the carrot fries to a bowl and drizzle with oil. Sprinkle with spices and seasoning. Toss to combine and arrange on the baking sheet.

3. Place in the oven and bake for 20 minutes.

4. In the meantime, combine the chopped chipotle, mayo, and lime juice in a small bowl.

5. Serve the cooked fries with the mayo.

Madras Curry Fries

The perfect side order to serve with curry and rice.

Servings: 2

Total Time: 1hour 30mins

Ingredients:

- 2 russet potatoes (peeled, cut into ½" fries)
- 4 tbsp vegetable oil
- 1 tsp Madras curry powder
- ½ tsp kosher salt
- ¼ tsp ground black pepper
- ¼ tsp garlic powder

Directions:

1. In a bowl, add the potatoes and cover with hot, not boiling, water. Soak for half an hour.

2. Preheat the main oven to 475 degrees F.

3. Using a colander, drain the fries and pat dry with kitchen paper.

4. Wipe the bowl clean before returning the fries to the bowl.

5. Add the curry powder followed by the salt, pepper and garlic power. Toss thoroughly to combine.

6. Transfer the fries, in a single layer to the baking sheet.

7. Cover tightly with aluminum foil and bake in the preheated oven for 5 minutes.

8. Remove the aluminum foil and continue baking for 12 - 15 minutes, or until the bottoms of the fries are golden.

9. Using tongs, flip the fries over, while keeping them in a single layer and return to the oven and cook for 10-15 minutes, until golden and crisp.

10. Transfer the golden fries to a kitchen towel-lined serving platter to absorb any excess oil and season.

11. Serve warm.

Mexican Fries with Salsa

No need for nachos, when you can whip up a batch of spicy fries. Serve with sour cream, guacamole, and cheese for a truly authentic Mexican flavor.

Servings: 2

Total Time: 40mins

Ingredients:

Salsa Ketchup:

- 3 tbsp tomato ketchup
- 3 tbsp salsa
- Hot sauce (to taste)

Fries:

- 1 tbsp olive oil
- 1 tbsp cornstarch
- ½ tsp salt
- ½ tsp garlic powder
- ¼ tsp pepper
- ¼ tsp ground cumin
- ¼ tsp chipotle chili pepper
- 2 medium russet potatoes (peeled, cut into ¼" fries)

Toppings:

- Sour cream
- Guacamole
- Grated cheese

Directions:

1. First, make the salsa. In a small bowl, whisk the ketchup with the salsa. Taste, adding additional salsa or ketchup according to your preference. Set aside.

2. Preheat the main oven to 400 degrees F. using parchment paper, line a baking sheet.

3. Add the oil, cornstarch, salt, garlic powder, pepper, cumin, and chili pepper to a large mixing bowl and whisk to incorporate. Add the fries and toss to evenly coat.

4. Arrange the fries, on the baking sheet and bake in the preheated oven for 20 minutes. Toss, stir and arrange into a single layer, cooking for a further 10 minutes.

5. Serve the cooked fries with the toppings and prepared salsa.

Parmesan Garlic Truffled Fries

Indulge yourself with these deliciously sophisticated fries flavored with garlic, Parmesan, and truffle oil.

Servings: 2-3

Total Time: 40mins

Ingredients:

- 2 Russet potatoes (skin-on, chopped into ¼-½" thick fries)
- 1 tbsp olive oil
- 1 tbsp truffle oil
- ¼ cup Parmesan cheese (grated)
- 1 tsp powdered garlic
- 1 tbsp parsley (minced)
- Sea salt and black pepper

Directions:

1. Preheat the main oven to 450 degrees F. Lightly grease a baking sheet.

2. Add the fries to a large bowl. Drizzle with the oils and toss to coat.

3. Sprinkle with the Parmesan cheese, powdered garlic, parsley, and seasoning. Toss again. Transfer to the baking sheet.

4. Place in the oven and bake for half an hour, until crisp. Allow to cool for a few minutes before serving.

Parsley and Lemon Fries

A simple French fries recipe using only a handful of ingredients is the perfect way to jazz up a meal.

Servings: 4-6

Total Time: 1hour 10mins

Ingredients:

- 6 russet potatoes (peeled, cut into ¼" fries)
- Virgin olive oil
- 1 cup parsley (chopped)
- Sea salt
- 2 lemon wedges (to squeeze)

Directions:

1. Add the fries to a cold water filled bowl and allow to soak for 10 minutes.

2. Drain, and arrange in a single layer on a parchment lined baking sheet. Drizzle with olive oil and sprinkle with parsley and sea salt.

3. Bake in an oven set at 375 degrees F for 40-45 minutes, until golden and cooked through, while remembering to move the fries around every 10 minutes or so.

4. Remove the fries from the oven and squeeze with lemon juice.

5. Season with additional salt to taste.

Pepperoni Pizza Fries

Our two favorite comfort foods in one dish; pizza and fries!
What's not to love!?

Servings: 3-4

Total Time: 45mins

Ingredients:

- 1 pound frozen crinkle-cut fries
- 1 cup tomato pizza sauce
- 1½ cups mozzarella cheese (shredded)
- 3 ounces pepperoni slices

Directions:

1. Cook the fries on a baking tray according to bag directions.

2. Pour the pizza sauce over the cooked fries and sprinkle with the cheese.

3. Arrange the sliced pepperoni on top.

4. Return to the hot oven for 5-6 minutes and bake until the mozzarella cheese melts.

5. Enjoy!

Pesto and Parmesan Wedges

These Italian style wedges are crispy on the outside and moist on the inside and combined with pesto and Parmesan are potato perfection.

Servings: 4

Total Time: 40mins

Ingredients:

- 6 medium russet potatoes (cut into wedges)
- Nonstick spray
- 2 tbsp virgin olive oil
- 4 tbsp ready-made pesto
- 3 tsp garlic (peeled, minced)
- 1 tsp sea salt
- ½ tsp black pepper
- ½ cup Parmesan (freshly grated)
- Kosher salt (to season)

Directions:

1. Add the wedges to a large bowl of cold water. The water needs to cover all of the potatoes. Soak for approximately 10 minutes.

2. Preheat the main oven to 475 degrees F. Lightly mist a baking tray with nonstick spray.

3. Using a colander, drain the wedges and pat dry with kitchen paper towel.

4. In a bowl, combine the oil with the pesto, followed by the garlic and seasonings. Add the wedges and gently toss to combine in the pesto evenly. Cover the bowl with aluminum foil.

5. Transfer to the oven and bake for several minutes. Remove the aluminum foil and bake for another 12-15 minutes, or until the wedges are sufficiently cooked through and fork tender.

6. Sprinkle with grated Parmesan and return to the oven to cook, for 2-3 minutes, or until the cheese melts.

7. Taste, season and enjoy.

Ranch Fries

An economical side order or snack using only two main ingredients.

Servings: 4

Total Time: 35mins

Ingredients:

- 3-4 russet baking potatoes (scrubbed, cut into ¼" fries)
- Nonstick spray
- 1 (1 ounce) ranch dressing mix

Directions:

1. Place the fries in a ziploc bag and lightly mist with nonstick spray, turning the bag to evenly coat.

2. Add half of the ranch mix, tossing to combine and repeat.

3. Arrange on baking sheet, lightly coated with nonstick spray.

4. Bake at 450 degrees F for 25-30 minutes, or until fork tender flipping over once.

5. Serve.

South of the Border French Fries

Green chili and cheese fries are a tasty snack to serve with drinks.

Servings: 4

Total Time: 45mins

Ingredients:

- 6 baking potatoes (peeled, cut into ¼" fries)
- 1 cup green chili sauce
- 1 cup cheddar cheese (grated)

Toppings:

- Sour cream
- Guacamole

Directions:

1. Bake the fries in the oven at 400 degrees F, for 15-20 minutes.

2. In a small pan, heat the chili sauce.

3. When the fries are sufficiently cooked, transfer to a pie pan, pour the chili sauce over the top and sprinkle with grated cheddar cheese.

4. Return to the oven for 4-6 minutes, or until the cheese has melted.

5. Serve with your favorite toppings.

Spicy Moroccan Sweet Potato Fries

Sweet potatoes seasoned with Moroccan spices are a welcome change from regular French fries.

Servings: 4-6

Total Time: 45mins

Ingredients:

- 2 medium sweet potatoes (peeled, cut into thin fries)
- 3-4 tsp olive oil
- 1 tsp ground cumin
- 1 tsp ground coriander
- ½ tsp ground ginger
- ¼ tsp ground turmeric
- ¼ tsp ground cinnamon
- 1 tsp salt
- ¼ tsp black pepper

Directions:

1. Arrange the sweet potato fries on a baking pan.

2. Drizzle with oil and scatter with the cumin, coriander, ginger, turmeric, ground cinnamon, salt, and pepper. Toss to evenly coat.

3. Bake at 400 degrees F for 40-45 minutes, or until golden and cooked through, flip over once halfway through cooking.

4. Enjoy.

Sweet Potato Fries with Maple Tahini Dip

Tahini is a sesame paste used widely in Mediterranean and Middle Eastern cooking, sweetened with maple syrup and season with garlic; it makes the perfect punchy dip for crispy sweet potato fries.

Servings: 4

Total Time: 45mins

Ingredients:

Fries:

- 4 sweet potatoes (peeled, cut into fries)
- ¼ cup virgin coconut oil
- Sea salt and black pepper

Tahini Dip:

- ½ cup tahini
- ¼ cup maple syrup
- 1 tbsp apple cider vinegar
- ¼ tsp powdered garlic
- Sea salt and black pepper

Directions:

1. Preheat the main oven to 375 degrees F. Cover a cookie sheet with parchment.

2. Add the fries to a large bowl, drizzle with coconut oil and season. Toss to coat.

3. Transfer to the cookie sheet.

4. Place in the oven and bake for just over half an hour, tossing halfway through cooking.

5. While the fries cook prepare the dip.

6. Combine the tahini, maple syrup, vinegar, garlic, and seasoning in a small bowl.

7. Serve the cooked fries with the dip.

Thai Curry Fries with Coconut Lime, Yogurt Dip

French fries are tossed in spicy Thai curry paste, baked until crispy and served with a cooling coconut, lime yogurt dip. Be sure to make plenty; these fries tend to disappear quickly!

Servings: 4

Total Time: 1hour

Ingredients:

Fries:

- 3 tbsp Thai green curry paste
- 1 tsp sea salt
- ¼ cup grapeseed oil
- 1¾ pound Russett potatoes (peeled, cut into ¼" fries)

Dip:

- ¼ cup plain full-fat yogurt
- 1 tbsp canned coconut milk
- 1 tsp fresh lime zest (grated)
- ½ tsp fresh lime juice
- 1 tsp honey
- Pinch cayenne pepper

Directions:

1. Preheat the main oven to 425 degrees F. Cover a baking sheet with parchment.

2. Combine the curry paste, salt, and oil in a small bowl.

3. Add the fries to a large bowl and pour over the curry paste mixture. Toss to coat and transfer to the baking sheet.

4. Place in the oven and bake for just over 45 minutes. Flip halfway through cooking.

5. In the meantime, prepare the dip.

6. Combine the yogurt, coconut milk, lime zest, juice, honey, and cayenne pepper in a small bowl. Chill until ready to serve.

7. Serve the cooked fries with the dip.

Two-Cheese Skillet French Fries

If you like cheese then these fries are for you; Cheddar and Monterey Jack come together for a super tasty, spicy nibble.

Servings: 4

Total Time: 55mins

Ingredients:

- 1 pound frozen French fries
- 1 cup Cheddar cheese (shredded)
- 1 cup Monterey Jack cheese (shredded)
- 10 slices cooked bacon (chopped)
- ¼ cup green onions (sliced)
- ¼ cup pickled jalapenos

Directions:

1. Preheat the main oven to 350 degrees F.

2. Cook the fries following the package instructions.

3. In an ovenproof skillet, add half of the fries and top with half of the Cheddar cheese and shredded Monterey Jack cheese, followed by the cooked bacon, sliced onions, and jalapenos.

4. Repeat the layering using the fries and toppings.

5. Bake in the oven until the cheese melts, this will take around 10 minutes.

Vinegar French Fries

Quintessentially British, French fries with salt and vinegar.

Servings: 4-6

Total Time: 1hour 35mins

Ingredients:

- 4 russet potatoes (washed, peeled, cut into ¼ "fries)
- 4 tbsp distilled white vinegar
- Vegetable oil (to fry)
- Kosher salt

Directions:

1. Add the fries to a bowl and cover with cold water, add 2 tbsp of white vinegar and transfer to the refrigerator for between 1-4 hours. This will enable the starch to turn into sugar which adds flavor to the dish.

2. Heat a Dutch oven, and pour in sufficient oil to fill a depth of no less than 3" and heat to 325 degrees F.

3. Using a colander, strain the fries and pat dry.

4. In batches, fry in the hot oil, using a spoon to avoid them sticking to one another. Cook until the fries are golden brown and fork tender, this will take around 4-5 minutes.

5. Transfer the fries to a wire baking rack and increase the temperature of the oil to 375 degrees F.

6. Return the fries to the oil and fry for 2-3 minutes more.

7. Toss the fries with the remaining white vinegar, and season with kosher salt.

8. Serve.

Yucca Fries

Yucca is more fibrous than a regular potato, and it's a good idea to cut it into thicker fries rather than sticks to make sure that it's crispy on the outside but moist on the inside.

Servings: 4

Total Time: 30mins

Ingredients:

- 3 cups canola oil
- 1 tbsp fine sea salt
- 1 tsp black pepper
- 1 tsp paprika
- 1 tsp cayenne pepper
- 2 pounds fresh yucca root
- Zest of 1 fresh lime

Directions:

1. Heat the oil, in a Dutch oven to 350 degrees F.

2. Add the salt, pepper, paprika and cayenne pepper to a large bowl, and mix to incorporate.

3. Remove the bark from the yucca by peeling with a heavy duty, strong veggie peeler. Cut the yucca into ¼" wide strips, approximately 4" in length.

4. Add the yucca to the oil and fry until golden. Using a slotted spoon, remove the yucca from the oil and drain off any excess oil using kitchen towel.

5. Season the fries with the spice mixture and zest and serve.

About the Author

Martha Stone is a chef and also cookbook writer. She was born and raised in Idaho where she spent most of her life growing up. Growing up in the country taught her how to appreciate and also use fresh ingredients in her cooking. This love for using the freshest ingredients turned into a passion for cooking. Martha loves to teach others how to cook and she loves every aspect of cooking from preparing the dish to smelling it cooking and sharing it with friends.

Martha eventually moved to California and met the love of her life. She settled down and has two children. She is a stay at home mom and involves her children in her cooking as much as possible. Martha decided to start writing cookbooks so that she could share her love for food and cooking with everyone else.

Author's Afterthoughts

Thank you for reading my book. Your feedback is important to us. It would be greatly appreciated if you could please take a moment to *REVIEW* this book on Amazon so that we could make our next version better

Thanks!

Martha Stone